TH
END OF WORDS

Issues in
Contemporary Quaker Theology

REX AMBLER

QUAKER HOME SERVICE
• LONDON •

First Published July 1994
reprinted June 1995
by
Quaker Home Service

ISBN 0 85245 262 4

Printed in *Friends House*, London.

CONTENTS

The end of words is to bring

men to a knowledge of things

beyond what words can utter.

Isaac Penington, *Letters*

PREFACE

This booklet arose from a series of talks I gave in Woodbrooke in the Summer of 1992. I had been asked to give eleven talks on *Some Issues in Quaker Theology Today*, so as to stimulate discussion and further study. I thought for some time about this. What issues should I deal with, and what issues could I deal with? There seemed to be so many worth discussing. Yet, on the other hand, the issues that I could think of all seemed to be linked together. The issue of whether we as Quakers were Christian, for example, seemed to be linked to what we believed about God, and that in turn was linked to the significance of referring to 'that of God in everyone' and the right we had to be optimistic about changing the world. I decided to resolve the puzzle - rather rashly, you might think - by gathering together all the important issues I was aware of and studying precisely what the links were between them. I had a hunch that understanding the links would help us considerably in understanding the issues themselves and possibly in resolving them as well. I feel fairly confident now, having gone through the course with the twenty five or so students who attended it, that the hunch was right.

The chapters as they now stand started out as short essays that I wrote for myself by way of preparation for the talks. The talks themselves were given extemporarily. However, the long discussions we often had after the talks, lasting sometimes for 3 or 4 hours, persuaded me to go back to my essays and revise them, or rewrite them completely. When a couple of students then asked if they could have copies of my notes, because they had missed one or more of the sessions, I told them I was presently rewriting them in the light of our discussions. This raised some interest in the group, and I soon found myself making copies available to all of them. I showed the text to some other Friends too, thinking they might be interested in the process and the clarification that came of it. Some of them were, and suggested publication. So, in the light of their comments and with further thoughts of my own, I revised the whole text yet again, to be suitable as a booklet. It is now much more carefully thought through than when it was first written. But I have retained some features of those first introductory essays: the brevity of each piece, the informal manner of writing and the highlighting of questions that need to be answered. I hope that in doing this I can also retain the original intention of the talks, which was to stimulate thought and discussion.

INTRODUCTION

1. Is theology the word?

Quakers have long been suspicious of theology, but it is not always clear that they have reason to be suspicious, or, if they have, that it is a good reason. If we take 'theology' in an older, popular sense, as a 'system of religious ideas', then no doubt there is a reason, and a good one. Quakers object in principle to the formulation of ideas as carrying authority, whether as 'notions' or as 'creeds'. But why? As soon as we ask this question we have to think more deeply about the rationale of Quaker attitudes and practices, and this leads us immediately into 'theology' in another sense of the word. This is theology as 'thinking about belief' so as to get a good understanding of it, or perhaps, 'talking and writing about belief' so as to gain a good mutual understanding. The point of this exercise is not to establish what we ought to believe on the basis of a given authority like the Bible, but to clarify what we already believe on the basis of experience. In a Quaker context this might mean, for example, trying to explain what is meant by 'the inner light' that we are committed to, why it implies a rejection of final authority in religion, and how it fits in with the rest of our beliefs and practices. Is this kind of theology more acceptable?

There is a view among Friends, though it is rarely articulated in this precise logical form, that even in this secondary role theology is unacceptable. The reasons would be that (1) it still gives too much weight to formulation in words, when what is important is always and only the experience and its outcome in action, (2) it relies too much on logic and reasoning, when what is being considered is beyond human thought, and (3) in formulating clear positions, precise interpretations, it provokes opposition and therefore tends to dissension and division. What is distinctive about Quakers is that in matters of the spirit they give priority to experience, allowing themselves to be guided by the deepest impulses within them, 'that of God' within them, rather than following ideas and beliefs which are only after all human constructions.

There is some truth in these objections. Words are finally inadequate to what we experience, especially in relation to what strikes us as ultimate and final. Reasoning, in the sense of giving logical shape to our words, has its limits. And when it is allowed to dominate our lives, to the exclusion of other ways of seeing and knowing, it is indeed oppressive and divisive. But it has to be said on the other side that we also need words and their careful, disciplined formulation, especially when it concerns our most deeply held beliefs and cherished insights. We need them to highlight what is most true for us and most worthwhile; to integrate the many different insights and values we already have, but which are often confused and at odds; to guide us in putting our beliefs into action; to communicate with one another about them so that we can support and correct one another and act together. Formulation of belief about the world in which we live, and about ourselves, is therefore actually necessary and beneficial. To resist formulation could even be harmful both to ourselves and to others, entailing repression or suppression of conflicts and uncertainties which need to be worked through.

But what then is the difference between formulating a belief and formulating a creed? They sound like the same thing. Indeed, and the point is crucial. And the difference helps to clarify the Quaker objection to creeds, and to the kind of theology that seeks to defend or elaborate a creed. A creed, we should remember, is a formulation of belief which is supposed to be valid in all times and places, and for everyone. What Quakers object to in their testimony against creeds is not formulation of belief as such, but giving one particular formulation authority over what people say and do, as if the ultimate mystery of life could be encapsulated once and for all in a particular set of words. Words and thoughts and reasons are not to be given that kind of trust, that kind of absolute confidence. Only God deserves that trust, and God is beyond all words and all forms. So our words, and all the beliefs we string out of them, are always, we insist, fallible, provisional, open to correction. And to indicate this fact in the way we use words about God - breaking the logic when reason comes to an end and letting poetry and metaphor intervene for example - could be part of our witness to the God who transcends them. Moreover, we who express ourselves in words are ourselves limited, and we change and differ among ourselves. Our beliefs about God and the world therefore - these grand gestures to a totality we can never comprehend - can only be working hypotheses, testable in the practice of our lives, but never finally capable of proof. (For further discussion see my *Creeds and the Search for Unity*, QHS, 1989, and Geoffrey Hubbard, *Quaker by Convincement*, QHS, 1985, part II 'Fundamental beliefs'.)

If this is the better expression of the Quaker view, it seems to suggest not only why one kind of theology is quite unacceptable, but also why and how another kind of theology could be possible and positively desirable. If the first kind of theology is intellectual stipulation, the second could be described as intellectual illumination. The first assumes that the relevant truth has already been revealed, in the distant past, and in an unambiguous verbal form that makes it accessible to reason. The task of theology is then to explain the meaning of what has been revealed in the past and to interpret its meaning for the new situation in which we live today. It is essentially a one-way process of interpretation, from the ancient text to the present-day reader. The second kind of theology, theology as intellectual illumination, assumes that the relevant truth is given in our human experience, initially in experiences 'beyond what words can utter', but then also in the words and actions and lives that bear witness to that inner revelation. The task of theology in this case is to interpret those many forms of witness, in the light of our own relevant human experience, so as to gain a fuller understanding of the truths being revealed. There can be no one-way interpretations here, but attention to many voices from many situations, past and present. Theology will be dialogue, open to light 'from whatever quarter it may come'. In a Quaker context of course it will be first of all dialogue between Friends, arising from their experience of meeting together, within the disciplines of their faith, and of their recollection of the tradition. Their theologizing together will try, among other things, to articulate what they are learning together and what together they have to say to the world. But since they have already learnt in their history to recognize 'that of God' in everyone else their theology could never be confined to an articulation of 'Quaker belief'. It would have to be aimed at a truth that was also true for everyone else; they would witness to the truth which they have found in their own experience and tradition, but, just in order to be faithful to that truth, they would also listen to the truth that others have to give, and in the hope that out of this dialogue a greater, fuller truth will be realized. Faced as we are, increasingly, with a great diversity of beliefs and experiences, often bewildering and sometimes worrying, we could say that theology was an attempt to take some intellectual responsibility in the situation and work towards a peaceful resolution of these spiritual conflicts, and towards a set of relationships in which the diversity can turn out to be mutually enriching.

I hope these proposals will prove to be helpful as we come to discuss the various specific issues that seem to call for theological reflection today. That is, I hope that in the writing and reading and discussion of the text we can do theology in a Quaker manner, and not merely on issues of Quaker concern.

IDENTITY

2. Quaker identity.

The issues to be discussed are what I understand to be points of actual concern or confusion in contemporary Quaker writing and talking. I am responding to what I hear is already being said, rather than attempting to initiate a discussion. At the same time I want to bring my own perspective to the issues, and in particular to introduce some theological discipline into the discussion by considering the issues in relation to one another and by placing the issues in the wider context of religious and cultural change.

Let me begin with a simple suggestion: that many of our present confusions arise from the impact of the unique Quaker protest against final authorities, which I discussed in the Introduction. This radical move created and still creates a number of difficulties for understanding.

1. It is negative, so it is not immediately apparent what Quakers positively affirm, and what positively they are committed to in practice.

2. It accepts diversity and individuality on principle, so it is difficult to see what Quakers themselves could have in common, agree on, establish as a basis of their Society.

3. In rejecting past authorities, we must ask, does it reject the authority of its own foundation? This applies as much to the authority of the Bible as to the authority of the founding fathers and mothers of Quakerism.

4. Its rejection of Christianity as it actually exists seems to rely on a deeper affirmation of Christian faith. Does that make it Christian? Can Quakers decide for themselves what 'Christian' means? (Cf. Humpty Dumpty's reply to Alice when she objected to his use of a particular word: 'When I use a word it means exactly what I say it means, no more and no less'!)

5. What Quakers claim for themselves they claim for everybody, that they have within them a potential for understanding what is

ultimately important to them and for living in the light of it. This in part is the basis of their nonviolent intervention in the affairs of the world. But since the world in general doesn't accept this view, how realistic is the Quaker intervention?

These questions set the themes for what follows: which as you see, I have divided into issues of identity, communication and action. The issue of identity seems a logical place to begin.

* * *

One of the results of not having a fixed form of faith is that it is difficult to determine how Quaker faith relates to other faiths, even Christian faith. In fact it is particularly difficult in relation to Christianity since that does formulate its faith in creeds and other identifiable structures. It seems that there is a lack of parity between Quakerism and every other form of Christianity, such that we cannot decide by comparison between them whether Quakerism is Christian. This was clearly a problem in our application to join the new Council of Churches for Britain and Ireland - I was involved in this process and found it, personally, quite painful. From our point of view it was incredible that the other churches should insist on agreement to a formal statement of belief as a condition of being accepted as Christian. From their point of view it was almost impossible to judge whether we were Christian or not since we refused to accept a creed or any other structure of authority that would define what 'Christian' meant. (We were accepted nevertheless because our corporate discipline and regard for the person of Jesus seemed to tie us into the Christian tradition, just.) If Christianity is to be defined by the majority view or by formal structures which most churches have in common Quaker-ism is not Christian. If on the other hand it is to be defined by its own self-understanding or self-identity it probably is Christian, or rather, capable of identifying itself as Christian. This is not so much a question of fact as a question of interpretation: given that we live in a time and place very different from that in which Christianity first arose, we have to come to a view - those of us who still take Christianity seriously - about what Christianity now means. In this respect Quakers are no different from everyone else. None of us can avoid interpretation. But Quakers are unusual in so far as their interpretation of Christianity has been radically different from that of most other people from the very beginning of their movement, and moreover, their emphasis on inwardness and individual freedom, against all objective norms, has been part of what they have taken Christianity itself to mean.

It must be admitted though that the majority, or those in power, have a distinct advantage. Their interpretation of Christianity will carry such weight that it will seem to be indisputable. A small and comparatively weak group like the Quakers, with a very different interpretation, will just for that reason be seen to be odd, contentious and highly disputable. Its claim to Christianity will be considered quaint at best. And this ambiguity will affect, and surely does affect, Quakers themselves, in that they too become uncertain as to whether and how to apply the Christian label, and what is worse, divided among themselves over whether or not they belong to Christianity.

So Quakers have problems in their relationship to the major religious tradition of the west because of (1) their untypical emphasis on inwardness and spiritual freedom, and (2) their smallness in numbers, which prevents them from making a significant mark in the wider world. But there is another difficulty, (3) the worldliness of Quakers, that is, their commitment to expressing faith primarily in a way of life in the world. As we shall see, this commitment to action is intimately connected with the emphasis on inwardness, but an obvious consequence is that to many people it hardly seems religious at all, let alone Christian. It seems more like a secularized version of Christianity, which therefore hardly deserves the name - and there may be some truth in that. But by the same token - because of their openness to the world - Quakers are unusually open to people of other faiths, which in a time of cultural and religious mix must inevitably affect the attitudes and practices of Quakers themselves. Some will be 'drawn' to Buddhism for example, others to the New Age. At one level this makes no difference, because the characteristic emphases on inwardness and way of life remain exactly as they were; but at another level it can cause confusion and distress, with some Quakers asserting the universality of religious truth and others, on the contrary, asserting the uniqueness of Christian truth in particular. This present dispute among Friends has something to do with the way they regard their own past.

3. Interpreting the Quaker past.

Our characteristic stress, being both mystical and practical, is concerned with the spiritual conditions of the actual moment. We do not lay special stress upon the authority of tradition, though with others we have regard to our past. We look rather to the living presence of the Spirit of God. This presence is known both as the individual is illumined by the light of Christ, and as the community is made aware of the same ever-present Holy Spirit. (*London Yearly Meeting Proceedings 1946,* pp. 82-3, quoted in LYM's *To Lima with Love,* 1987, p.5)

For a society that emphasises openness to present experience and insights 'from whatever quarter they may come' it may be surprising that it remains so preoccupied with its own past, and in particular with the figure of George Fox. On further reflection, though, it can be seen that something like this is necessary for retaining a sense of identity and unity within the society. In place of a bible or a hierarchy we have 'early Friends'! Or do we? There is a problem here - and a real diversity of opinion. The problem is that if we allow Fox and Co. authority over our present way of thinking and living we are negating the very principle that Fox and Co. stood for, the priority of one's own spiritual leadings. But if we don't give them authority we would seem to have no objective reference for determining what counts as Quaker, what defines the society. For example, if someone disagreed with my account of the 'principle' that Friends stood for and stand for, 'the priority of one's own spiritual leadings', how would we settle this disagreement? Another version of this problem concerns the use we make of distinctive Quaker language, most of which belongs unmistakably to the 17th century. We speak of 'following the light', 'greeting that of God' in everyone, doing things 'in right ordering' and so on. We even reiterate the famous question, 'What canst *thou* say?'. We often use language like this to give weight to what we say, to indicate that this is indisputable common ground, and to express our continuity and solidarity with the Friends who started our movement. But in speaking like this we also lean on what others have said, from their experience, rather than speaking directly from our own. The point can be put ironically: 'Fox said this, and Fell said that, but what canst thou say?'

One side of the debate (e.g. the New Foundation Group) resolves the problem by (re)defining the principle of Quaker faith as obedience to the light of Christ, as previously revealed in George Fox and the Bible. Lewis Benson, who has been most influential in developing this view, made this point in an article on 'The Relation of Quakerism to its own History' (*Quaker Religious Thought*, vol.III, no.2, Autumn 1961, p.29):

> I believe that it is essential to the life of Quakerism that it keep a right relation to its own history. The experience of hearing and obeying, although it must always be an experience of hearing God's voice "while it is today", is nonetheless an experience of a voice which has been speaking in every age.

Freedom of thought, difference in personal experience and changing circumstances are therefore all irrelevant. All that matters is that we continue to hear and obey the one voice, with its one message, that has spoken to and through faithful people throughout the ages, from Moses and Jesus to the present day.

The other side of the debate resolves the problem by defining the Quaker principle as an acceptance of a universal truth which is essentially mystical: that is, it is a truth of our deep unity with God which cannot be expressed adequately in words and which, when it is expressed, nearly always comes out differently. In fact, on this interpretation the difference in expression could be celebrated, since it helps us to find a unity which is not based on words, but precisely on the experience that is 'beyond what words can utter'. We will find unity with early Friends not in repeating their phrases, but in recognizing in what they say, and maybe more in what they do, the same indefinable spirit. By the same token we should find unity and fellowship with people of other faiths, however remote they may be culturally. This view was pioneered by another American Quaker, Rufus Jones, who reflected the new wave of liberal Christianity at the beginning of the century. He saw Quakerism as one manifestation among many of a type of religion he called 'spiritual', as opposed to religions that were authoritarian or rationalist. What Quakers did, he claimed,

> ...was to insist that religion is something that begins within the soul of man. They passed over, as Copernicus did, to a new centre. This change of centre underlay Luther's new interpretation of faith, but Luther failed to go all the way through with his reforming idea. He stopped midway. What Friends aimed to do was to ground religion for ever upon an inherent relation between God as living Spirit and the elemental spiritual nature of man. Religion, they believed, does not rise outside and flow in; it springs up inside and flows out. It is not primarily concerned with books, documents, creeds or institutions. It is rather concerned with the awakening of a divine urge in the utmost deeps of the self. (*The Faith and Practice of the Quakers,* 1927, pp.39f.)

But they added to the longstanding tradition of spiritual or mystical religion the idea that each person has to test this truth for him or her self, in harmony with the then new scientific method.

> Experience, then is the Quaker's starting-point. This light must be my light, this truth must be my truth, this faith must be my very own faith.... They come back for their basis to the test of experience - to the laboratory of life. (*Ibid.* pp.47,52.)

As compared with the first view, this more liberal view has been called 'universalist', although, as we shall see, that may not be the best word for making the distinction. In this context I would rather contrast the two symbols that emerged in those quotations from Benson and Jones. The dominant symbol for Benson is 'voice', for Jones it is 'light'. A voice speaks, and its meaning must be understood and heeded. A light shows, but what it shows is open to interpretation, and people may differ in what they say they can see.

It seems to me, however, that although both views have much to commend them, neither view resolves the problem satisfactorily. They both present Quakerism as a type of something else, some other more general spirituality. The theology of the voice presents it as a form of Christianity which gives priority to the 'word' of God, rather as Luther did. In fact Benson himself leans very heavily on neo-orthodox protestant theologians like Emil Brunner and G. Ernest Wright, who were attempting to revive Luther's thought. Jones on the other hand was aligning Quakerism not only with the mystical tradition of the past but also with the prevalent 'liberal' Christianity of his own time, against which Brunner and Wright were to react so strongly. Quaker 'light' is then not so far from the liberal 'light of conscience' and 'light of reason'. I would suggest then that what Quakers have done is to recapitulate within their own movement the drama of modern Christianity: their present conflict over 'Christocentric' and 'universalist' interpretations of their faith echoes the recent conflict - now less evident - in the wider Christian movement over 'conservative' and 'liberal' interpretations, though happily without the more virulent third contestant of fundamentalism! What is happening here, I believe, is that Quakers have allowed themselves to be defined and identified, once again, by reference to some other wider movement, with which in fact they have significant differences.

I would suggest that Quakers rather try to define themselves and the movement of which they are a part in terms of their own distinctive way of speaking and way of doing things. They have started something new, which had not in this form existed before. And this new way of life, though it draws on many sources and influences, has an integrity of its own. As we know, or should know, from our own experience of the Society, it is held together in practice by a discipline of communal life. We have a discipline of silence, of collective decision-making, of attending to ministry and concern, of acting together, of simple and nonviolent lifestyle - and these different aspects of the discipline mutually support one another. It is this distinctive practice, I would say, that early Friends bequeathed to us, and which still now gives the clearest indication of what Quakerism is. The implications of this view we shall have to explore at another time.

4. Interpreting the historical Jesus.

I would suggest a similar approach to the historical Jesus, so as to overcome another issue among Friends about whether and how they believe in Christ, and about whether and how they use the Bible. Once again, the issue is shaped (unhelpfully) by the dominant forms of religion in our (western) society. Religious faith is given public definition by adherence to the word of the Bible (interpreted literally or otherwise) and by a relationship with Christ understood as a presently living being, precisely as witnessed to in the Bible. To be more specific, Christ is understood as a perfect and unique union of God and man - the man Jesus of Nazareth who was united with God (more strictly the eternal Son of God, who is nonetheless equal in Godhead with the Father), died a human death by execution, and came to life again two days later, to continue to live everlastingly 'with God' in heaven. As such the god-man Christ is the only mediator between God and humans, the only 'saviour' of humans from their basic human plight. To trust in Christ, this exalted being sent by God the Father, is the only hope humans have of attaining their own destiny or fulfilment. (The best image of this orthodox Christian faith is probably still the Gothic church, with its pews lined up facing the screen, behind which is the priest, the altar and the stained glass window pointing to a glory beyond.)

Accordingly, the rejection of religion in our society is mostly understood as a rejection of this kind of belief, and it is usually made on the ground that such belief is discredited, irrelevant or possibly harmful (psychologically and/or morally). When Friends are caught up in this affair (it is no longer an argued debate) they are bound to cause confusion and indeed to become confused themselves. For example, they are no longer, most of them, comfortable with talk of 'the Christ within' as the clue to what they are after, the 'teaching of the Bible' as the basis for what they do, or belief in the existence of God as the *sine qua non* for rationality, sanity or the practice of a good life. To that extent they have been influenced by the modern attitude which is suspicious of traditional authority in matters of faith and life. Or to put it another way round, we could say that Friends have been caught up in a movement which they themselves helped to initiate, encouraging people to trust in their own experience and their own judgment in every sphere of life, from science and politics to religion and philosophy, but which has since taken a direction that Friends didn't want.

Friends were, and are, different from other 'moderns': while emphasising the resources of the individual human self, against a dependence on authority, they did not claim that the individual person was self-sufficient. People were to look to their own experience in order to find 'that of God', something that quite transcends their own immediate thoughts and feelings. Christian faith was therefore not abandoned but transformed. It was turned from a cosmic drama of salvation, spanning human history, into an individual drama of experience. The great external events of God's history with men and women, as told in the Bible, were *internalized*. The creation of humans in innocence, the fall of humans into sin and despair, the appearance of Christ as prophet and saviour, the liberation from sin and evil, and the hope of glory in the kingdom of God - all these great events were now to be experienced within human beings. This impressed George Fox in particular:

The living light of Christ manifesteth all things; and the spiritual fire trieth all things.... These things are to be found in a man's heart. But to speak of these things being within seemed strange to the rough and crooked and mountainous ones. (*Journal of George Fox*, ed. John Nickalls, pp.15f.)

The Lord showed me that the natures of those things which are hurtful without were within, in the hearts and minds of wicked men. The natures of dogs, swine, vipers, of Sodom and Egypt, Pharaoh, Cain, Ishmael, Esau, etc. Those natures I saw within, though people had been looking without. (*ibid.* p.19.)

Now I was come up in spirit through the flaming sword into the paradise of God. All things were new, and all the creation gave another smell unto me than before, beyond what words can utter. I knew nothing but pureness and innocency, and righteousness, being renewed up into the image of God by Christ Jesus, so that I say I was come up into the state of Adam which he was in before he fell. (*ibid.* p.27.)

Douglas Gwyn has drawn attention to this theme in his excellent book on Fox's theology, *The Apocalypse of the Word* (Friends United Press, 1986):

Fox was able to discern two powers operative within himself - the fleshly power of his own thoughts and will, and the spiritual power of Christ's revelation and will. Fox came to know an apocalyptic battle within himself between Christ's power and Satan's. With this battle, his own redemption and that of the creation hung in the balance. (p.61)

He concludes the discussion of this theme as follows:

While most of his contemporaries looked to geo-political events for the much-expected apocalypse, George Fox found its beginnings revealed upon an inner landscape. (*ibid.* p.64.)

One implication of this new vision is that external events become less important, and, most significantly for Christian understanding, the external events on which the historic Christian drama was supposedly based are no longer as necessary as they were, and perhaps not necessary at all. This implication has not often been drawn by Friends, but now that the biblical construction of those events is increasingly in doubt historically it becomes increasingly important not to have our faith and hope tied up with them. It should not be at all necessary for example, to believe in the historical Jesus' rising from the dead when the spiritual significance of the story is perceived to be the possibility of our own inner experience of resurrection.

This severing of the historical Jesus from the experience of liberation can itself have a liberating effect on our understanding. We can, on the one hand, appreciate much more fully the *human* experience of Jesus who, as Fox liked to say, was inspired by the same spirit that moves us, only more so. On the other hand we are free to see the image of Christ as a symbol of our own profound experience - or, if the image doesn't seem to fit any more, to get along without it. If it does fit, I would suggest it could have one of two possible meanings. Christ could be either a symbol of transforming power within our own psyche, rather as Carl Jung interpreted it, or, alternatively, as an image of human possibility inspired by the historical Jesus. I would myself prefer the second option, but I see no reason to settle for one interpretation only. With all of them, however, including others I have not described and the option of not using the image at all, it is possible for Friends to think of the historical Jesus as a Brother rather than as a Lord, a real human being with whom we can identify, rather than as a supernatural god-man on whom we have to depend.

COMMUNICATION

5. Images of God.

What I have said so far might suggest that the less we say about God and the content of our belief the better! This is only partly true. The Quaker emphasis - which I am, I think, re-emphasising - is on what words cannot adequately express: the depth of our human experience and creative resources, the hidden bonds of community, the attention and action that develop those resources and nurture those bonds. This, among other things leads us to value silence, not saying and not doing. But strangely enough, it also seems to help us when we come to think about the meaning of our faith, as we do now, because what we have to think about is not first of all a set of words, but a common experience and practice. Theology is for us, then, not an interpretation of authoritative words, but a shared reflection of what we do and what we experience. This is the half truth.

The other half is that to sustain ourselves as a community, and in society at large, we need to communicate with one another. To share experiences, check individual biases, take up concerns, teach and learn - to do all this we have to convey in words what is of most concern to us. Hence also Quaker verbosity! We may claim that by comparison with other religious talk Quaker talk is free, spontaneous, 'deep', contextual, experiential, fallible, broken and personal; and that all this is embodied and safeguarded in our structures of ministry and decision-making. This is true, or may be a good part of the time. But it is also true that what is said needs to be understood, that sharing experiences requires a shared understanding, that community includes a vision of what we are all after.

There can be no doubt that the word 'God' represents what we as Quakers are after, even if some of us are not at all happy with the use of that word. So here is our first problem of communication. How do we communicate what is of ultimate importance to us when the traditional word for conveying it is, or seems, no longer viable? This problem is rather deeper than the ones we have looked at so far, because it is far more than a matter of how we relate to the past or the teachings of other religious bodies. Here is our own favoured word, rooted in tradition of course and very widely used by other people, but it is also our word and a word we have given special meaning to. On the other hand the difficulties in using and *meaning* that word today are very serious, and not to be taken lightly. We cannot discuss all the difficulties here, but let me hazard an account of what the central difficulty is.

The basic image of God, in the west, is the image of an all-powerful fatherly being, who created the world at the beginning of time, steers the world through its course according to his own chosen purpose, and faithfully helps those who turn to him for help. As a father is to an ancient tribe so God is to the world. But this idea has been seriously challenged in the last few hundred years as human beings have learnt to take control of the world themselves. The sons have rebelled against the father, and more recently the daughters have too. They have taken over the role that once they ascribed to the father, and now the father is seemingly redundant. This is a metaphor, of course, but I think it touches the deeper level of changes that have taken place since the rise of modern science and modern democracy, which has so deeply affected religion.

In more technical terms we should describe this process as secularization, and the present prevalent culture as *secularism*. Friends share that culture, so like everyone else they find little if any use for the word 'God' in everyday life. In everyday life - to put it simply - people have to believe in themselves, not in something or someone else. They may be 'religious' in the sense that they attend a religious group, but they are not expected to practise their religion conspicuously in the public sphere. Religion is essentially, in the west, a private option. Because of this it has become possible for people to attend a great variety of religious groups, to exercise their characteristically modern freedom to choose the religion they want. But this new *pluralism* of belief and practice has added to the general feeling that religion cannot be dealing with objective reality, with how the world is in fact, but only with stories and myths which express perhaps how people feel about the world. Since Quakers do not encourage the telling of stories that are remote from everyday life, but insist on the contrary that the stories we have to tell are those that we ourselves are involved in, it is doubly difficult for them to speak confidently of God. When they do speak of God they will often be heard to qualify the word with a phrase that recognizes the difficulty: 'God or whatever we may choose to call it'. Does this mean that they are fudging? The use of the word 'it' certainly sounds like it.

It might even be making a gesture towards some modern alternative to the traditional image of God, like 'the life force', 'cosmic consciousness', 'the unconscious' or 'the ground of being'. But this is not necessarily the case. It could be saying that what we call it is not really as important as the fact that we are pointing beyond ourselves and all known persons and things to the strictly unthinkable reality that yet gives them meaning. God cannot be pointed at, only towards, we might say.

But this characteristic Quaker phrase, and all the other hedging and fudging that Quakers may go in for, may also be marking the shift in consciousness brought about by *feminism*. This is confronting us, perhaps more powerfully than ever before, with the far-reaching implications of talking of God as person. A person is a 'she' or a 'he', never an 'it'. So if God is a person, God is either male or female. And now we are discovering just how male we have always perceived God to be, and how that in its turn has served to underwrite the superiority and dominance of human males throughout history. Is this perhaps why men have insisted so strongly over the years on the personal 'He' of God? It is an alarming thought. All this seems to add to the argument that we should altogether stop talking about God as a being of some sort, an imaginable entity, whether male or female, personal or impersonal, and bring our language back to the experience and practice where it really belongs. God is part of a story we tell about ourselves in order to convey something of the depth and mystery and creative power that we experience among ourselves and that we are hoping to trust and act upon in the conduct of our lives. God is a metaphor for the kind of reality that cannot be talked about directly and literally, certainly not in scientific language, or in rational philosophy either. But it is not a metaphor that we absolutely need for experiencing and responding to the reality it is supposed to be referring to. It is after all only a word.

6. Communicating faith.

Given our suspicion of language for the communication of faith, it might be expected that we should express some enthusiasm about art and music and other symbolic forms. These are widely recognized to be ways of communicating experiences which are beyond the reach of normal or rational language. (I leave aside, for the moment, the language of poetry and fiction, which have their own symbolic power, derived partly, I would say, from their breaking the rules of normal language.) People of other faiths use these forms freely, and precisely in order to get beyond words. But we Quakers obviously don't. On the contrary, we go as far as it is seemingly possible to go in order to avoid the symbolic representation of what we believe in or feel committed to. We have no altar or crucifix, no pulpit, pictures or stained-glass windows, no incense or sacraments, no hymns, introits or musical accompaniments. Instead we sit in silence in a bare-as-possible room, facing one another and an unadorned table, in a conscious, cultivated simplicity. Why? What are we trying to achieve by this? How do we manage to communicate, if we do, the deep realities we say we are concerned with? And have we perhaps misunderstood, and therefore failed to appreciate, the power and value of artistic symbols?

Two points could be made, and often are made, in response to this, but they seem to me to go not quite far enough. It could be said that what symbols do essentially is to give expression to feeling, and sometimes to arouse feeling, whereas Quaker worship is aimed at something deeper than that, a point of rest and stillness which is purely spiritual. The objection to symbols in worship is therefore akin to the objection to creeds and binding forms of belief, which we discussed in the first session: that they fail to take us beyond 'forms' and 'notions' to where spiritual reality is to be found. Part of this objection may be that feelings not only fall short of spirituality, but positively get in the way of it, by e.g. distracting our attention and awakening our desire. The Puritans were fond of this objection to the arts, but they tended to see human feelings, especially sexual feelings, as actively opposed to spirituality. Quakers in the past seem to have taken over this Puritan objection, with its asceticism and dualism, although it is difficult to find any good (Quaker) reason for their doing so.

The other point often made is that artistic forms in worship tend to be fixed and inflexible. The official Quaker document *To Lima with Love* (1987) - a response to the World Council of Churches publication on this theme, *The Lima Text* - makes the point in its discussion of baptism and the eucharist:

> Although our practice appears very different, we recognise many of the spiritual aspirations expressed in the symbolism of the eucharist... Nevertheless it is our experience that the grace of God is not restricted to any particular form of eucharistic liturgy.... We would assert that the validity of worship lies not in its form but in its power, and a form of worship sincerely dependent on God, but not necessarily including the words and actions usually recognised as eucharistic, may equally serve as a channel for this power and grace. (pp.9f.)

It quotes London Yearly Meeting's statement of 1928, describing the Friendly equivalent to the eucharist:

> In silence, without rite or symbol, we have known the Spirit of Christ so convincingly present in our quiet meetings that his grace dispels our faithlessness, our unwillingness, our fears, and sets our hearts aflame with the joy of adoration. We have thus felt the power of the Spirit renewing and recreating our love and friendship for all our fellows. This is our eucharist and our communion. (*ibid.* p.10)

Both texts give an irenic objection to the eucharist in the context of an ecumenical dialogue. They are concerned to affirm what other Christians are doing while at the same time giving a defensible account of what Quakers do differently. But the playing down of difference can also be confusing. It gives the impression that, by comparison with others, what Quakers do is essentially the same, but that they have no need of the same forms and structures to do it. To which eucharistic Christians may well reply, 'Surely that is your loss not ours!' If eucharist and baptism are not essentially out of place, but only unnecessary, they could on occasion perhaps be useful.

What is missing from these accounts is the essential difference in what we do. Orthodox Christians are looking beyond themselves to the personal being which is their creator and father, and they are looking to him to take the initiative in restoring their failing human relationship with him. The decisive action has already been taken, they believe, in God's intervention in the world in the life, death and resurrection of Christ. But now the benefits of this action in the past have to be received today; they have to be mediated to those who are waiting to receive them, which is precisely where the sacraments come in. In a symbolic form they bring the death-and-resurrection-of-Christ into the present moment, baptism signifying an identification with Christ in his dying and rising, and the eucharist signifying the gift of his broken body to those who wish to receive him. Without them the saving benefit of Christ's suffering would simply not be available. So, from the viewpoint of traditional Christian faith the sacraments are not optional, they are absolutely necessary.

Quakers, however, are not looking beyond themselves in this sense. They are looking within. The reality that can bring them to God, they believe, is within their own being, difficult though it may be to find and even more difficult to respond to. The dynamics of responding to this inner light or voice may be described in Christian terms, even in terms of dying and rising with Jesus, as we have seen, but the response always remains our response to what *we ourselves* are experiencing. The truth we are trying to confront, the truth that we believe will set us free, is always a truth that is staring us in the face, coming at us from our everyday experience of life, in both its suffering and renewal. And this is why we need stillness and silence. In our meetings for worship nothing needs to be 'mediated', because the presence is already with us, in our simple, scarred humanity. To give it our attention, and to allow everyone in the meeting to confront it in their own way, as they have to, but in the hope that eventually we might be able to confront it together, as a community, we screen out everything that might distract us. What we hope for, and wait for, is the experience of *immediacy*.

Rufus Jones was right to emphasise that - in the quotation I gave before, in part 3 - the early Quakers 'passed over, as Copernicus did, to a new centre'. Whereas before, the world had revolved around an objective God, above and beyond them, it was now seen to revolve around them, humble human beings as they were.

With this understanding we should be able to affirm both the necessity of silence and stillness and nonrepresentation, at the point of worship, and also the necessity of creative forms, at other times, which communicate the insights gained in worship. We should be able to say yes *and* no. As formed 'in the image and likeness of God' we can then, like God, create worlds. We can give expression to our insights, hopes, longings, feelings, sufferings, victories and whatever else, and in whatever expressive form we choose. In that respect Quakers could be, if they wished to be, exuberantly artistic.

7. Dialogue with people of other faiths.

All of us have difficulty in understanding and accepting the great variety of religious beliefs and practices in the world. In particular we have difficulty in communicating with people of other faiths than ours because our own customary language soon becomes inadequate. It is sometimes said though that Friends have less difficulty than most because they do not formulate their beliefs in a once-for-all statement or creed which others can agree with or disagree with. True religion, it is said, is not in the words, the forms, but in the inner experience.

So it is quite possible, on this view, that people of different verbal confessions may nevertheless have the same experience, and therefore have in common what is ultimately most important. Some Friends go further and argue that the same experience will be found behind all religions, providing a universal bond between all religious differences. Inter-faith dialogue would therefore be based on a common recognition of 'where words come from'.

However, it cannot be quite as easy as that, as we can see from a moment's reflection. As soon as we try to identify the common experience as a basis for discussion, we should find we were having to formulate an understanding of religious experience that could be considered fundamental to everyone involved, the Hindu, the Muslim, the Christian and the Jew. We should be very unlikely to succeed, given the very different ways we all have of talking about experience, but if, despite all obstacles, we were to succeed we should have stumbled across a verbal definition of true religious experience, a genuinely ecumenical creed! As a further embarrassment, to Quakers at least, we should find we have included within our universal definition religious beliefs and practices which we would otherwise find wholly unacceptable, e.g. beliefs and practices which promoted violence, terror or oppression. In such cases it would be quite wrong to suppose that we were basically in agreement, but differed only on matters of practice.

It would be better then to observe the Quaker suspicion of formal belief as a basis for unity, and look for the basis elsewhere. We could suggest that the basic experience that we believed different people share should remain *un*formulated, and simply acknowledged as a mysterious and finally inexpressible common ground. Such commonality, it would be agreed, can sometimes be felt, and glimpses of other people's experience can sometimes be gained through poetic illusion or well-told stories (following the ideas of the last chapter). What is needed is simply that people involved in an inter-faith dialogue should recognize this depth of experience and accept it as the true source of their respective (distinctive) religious insights. They may not then reach universal agreement - indeed such a thing would be intrinsically unlikely - but they would be able to communicate genuinely and helpfully. And Friends, it might be said, are especially well-placed to facilitate such dialogue because they are already committed to this inner religious experience and truth and they are not hindered by outward forms and objective authorities. In this respect they do not suffer the disability of other Christians who give the Bible or Christ or the Church such final authority that it is impossible for them to accept people of other faiths on equal terms.

But before we get thoroughly complacent on this issue we should recognize another difficulty in that reference to 'final authority' in the other Christian churches. We have difficulty communicating with other Christians on just this point: they accept an objective authority in religion, we do not. End of argument, end of dialogue. Friends, apparently, are not so flexible. The rejection of authority as absolute is part of their own faith and confession - which in this respect, we might wryly suggest, adds up to an anti-creed. They may of course also affirm the validity of others' inner experience, but this will not provide the basis for discussion, genuine common ground, because the others do not accept inner experience as the source of truth and goodness. There is a theological stalemate here, which is one of the things that has helped to keep Quakers at arm's length from the other churches for most of their 300 year history.

The same dilemma, of course, will show itself in Quaker relations with people of almost every other faith, since very few of them have the Quaker understanding of inner human experience. So have we reached a dead end?

Not quite, I think. There is another way of acknowledging the unity of human beings which does not depend on their having to agree on the nature of reality and experience. This is to say that all human beings have within them the capacity for mutual recognition, that is, the capacity to respond to other human beings as worthy of their care. And the unity achieved, when it is achieved, would be a unity of mutual care and co-operation. The main task and interest of dialogue would then be to achieve this mutual recognition so that we can better live together and help one another. It would be practical, more than theoretical. Theoretical understanding might later be possible as a reflection on our experience of interaction, and as such it would be invaluable. So far as I can see - and more importantly, on the basis of my own (limited) experience of interaction with people of other faiths - this approach would harmonize with the interests of most other religions. Not every one might 'agree' that, for example, the basic commandments are to love God and to love your neighbour as yourself, for each has their own way of speaking about these ultimates of experience, but Jews and Christians should be able to recognize in their practical dealings with Buddhists, Hindus and others that they show those commitments in their lives. Talk of 'God' and 'love' may be important for the Christian or the Jew in *their* way of describing the insight-cum-commitment, because these words are central to their culture. But they are not universal, though what they describe may well be.

What I am recommending then is a more modest form of universalism - and one which is not necessarily at odds with a Christo-centric view of Quakerism. It is what I would call a universalism of potential, since what it affirms is the potential of all human beings to realize their unity with other human beings, and with them a unity with God. This is not to say that all human beings realize this in fact, nor even that religions do, since religions in practice may distort or suppress human spirituality. And finally, it does not claim that actual religious experience will always be essentially the same. The recognition of how *different* they all are may, on the contrary, be increasingly important to a dialogue in which we seriously hoped to understand one another better. But the condition for this better understanding, and, I would think, the over-riding concern of inter-faith dialogue today, would have to be the mutual recognition of human beings, in their common earthly home, struggling to live together in some peace. Quakers could be whole-heartedly commit-ted to this process because it harmonizes with what they believe about the practical, worldly nature of 'true religion', but precisely because the process is initially practical they wouldn't have to gain agreement first of all about the nature of 'true religion'. And in this process the Quaker art of mediation and the nonviolent resolution of conflict may be far more significant than the Quaker belief in the priority of experience.

Appendix on universalism

My talk of a universalism of potential is only one interpretation of universalism. There are others, which have different implications for inter-faith relations. Perhaps it would be helpful if I listed what I think are the four main interpretations of universalism. They are often confused, unfortunately, not least in the minds of Quakers when they are trying to sort out the difference between 'Christo-centric' and 'universalist' interpretations of Quakerism itself. All these views have been described at one time or another as 'universalist':

1. On the mildest and most cautious interpretation, universalism is the belief that every human being, in whatever religion or culture, has the potentiality for true religious experience, although he or she may not in fact realize it. On this view it is possible to regard some religious movements or cultures as having quite failed to realize the human potential, and possibly as actively oppressing it. This, I think, would be Fox's view of the established Christianity of his time. (This is also the general view I am recommending, but with a practical twist.)

2. A stronger view is that every religion does in fact realize this potential for true religious experience, at least in its 'core' or essence. But it claims also that this experience is identifiably the same in every case, that it can be uncovered and rescued even where the outward forms of a religion conceal it or distort it. In this way Christianity and Hinduism could be said to have the same experience of the divine at the centre but also to express the experience in very different ways, largely because they have arisen in vastly different cultures.

3. Beyond this it can be claimed that the primary expressions of faith in every religion are the same. Arnold Toynbee once formulated this sameness as the command to love God and one's neighbour: there is on the one hand an act of faith in or dependence on the ultimate reality which is able to free a person from selfishness, on the other hand there is the ethic of acting on this faith in the unselfish care of the neighbour. On this account there is, then, in fact one universal religion, though it is dressed in many different ways. (In practice this view is confined to the so-called 'great world religions' and leaves out the 'primary' or tribal religions.)

4. The strongest view is that everyone will eventually reach God, 'be saved', attain eternal life, whatever their present mode of consciousness or religious attachment. This view could incorporate the previous views, holding that 'all paths lead to God', or, in a more pessimistic mood, it could maintain that all or most religions are deluded and that human beings will come to the truth only after this life. A Christian version of this holds that in a life after death, or in 'purgatory', everyone will finally turn to Christ. There are then universalisms of potential, of experience, of belief, and of salvation. It may be helpful to bear these possible interpretations in mind when we come to think how Quakers in particular might be universalist. They could surely adopt any one of these positions, or any combination of them, without being notably un-Quakerly. A Christo-centric Quaker would only find difficulty with the third position, I would imagine - the universalism of belief - because it seems to downgrade what is special to Christianity. So what after all is the fuss between Christo-centrics and universalists really about? Is it perhaps based on a misunderstanding?

ACTION

8. Making peace in the world.

Our reflection on the practical impetus of 'true religion' leads us into the last general theme for our discussion, the question of action in the world. There should be no problem, for Quakers, as to whether action in the world is appropriate for religious faith. On the contrary, we could say that for Quakers faith *impels* them into the world. 'True godliness', said William Penn, 'don't turn men out of the world, but enables them to live better in it, and excites their endeavours to mend it' (1682). This impulse or 'excitement' has to do with the affirmation of humans at the heart of our faith, which makes other humans always significant for our own spiritual development.

The problem, if there is one, has to do with the manner of our interventions in the world: not the *that* or the *whether* but the *how*. The question could be put like this: given the Quaker vision of what society could be and should be, how are Quakers in particular to act so as to help bring it about? There are some prior questions, no doubt, about what this Quaker vision is supposed to be, and whether Quakers have any agreement on it. But I have something quite simple in mind, which seems to me to correspond to the simple insight on which Quakers are working. The insight is that what we have discovered about ourselves and one another in relation to our own resources for dealing with the challenges of life applies to everyone we come into touch with. Everyone, we believe - and it has to be a matter of faith, rather than knowledge - has within them the potential to become what they are intended to be, both as individuals and as members of society. This is not to deny the potential also for evil and destructiveness. On the contrary, it is precisely because of the negative potential and its actual realizations in society and history that we need to engage in a spiritual struggle to overcome it. Quaker hope for the success of this struggle is not based on naive optimism about the essential goodness of human nature - or if it is, it is surely ill-founded - but on the availability of resources for dealing with what may be deeply ingrained habits of destructiveness, whether in individuals or society. And these resources are supposed to tap the sources of life itself, the creative power that makes life itself possible. This is only another way of saying what Quakers have always in fact said, though often without noting the full sense, that what we ultimately trust in is not ourselves but 'that of *God*' within us, and within everyone else. God, for us, is humanly mediated, which implies, paradoxically, that God is always *im*mediately available. So our expectations of what human beings can do and become is finely balanced between a sense of their great potential for love and sensitivity and justice on the one hand, and a sense of their all too human reluctance to realize it. I say 'reluctance' rather than 'inability' because the faith is, as I judge it, that we always have some choice in this matter, and that in the long run this choice is decisive. In our more traditional language, we would say that the 'light' of God is given to people, to make them at least dimly aware of who and where they are, but that whether and how they respond to this light is finally up to them.

I have been labouring this point because it seems to me to be necessary for an appreciation of the Quaker vision of society. The vision is neither purely utopian nor quietist. That is to say, it neither expects human beings to become wholly good and just so that the deepest problems of society will be finally overcome, nor does it on the other hand despair of the world, focusing narrowly on the community of faith, in the hope of some future intervention into the world by God. (In the past perhaps Friends have veered towards one or other of these, responding to the situation of the time.) But there is, we could say, a utopian possibility, because our experience tells us that humans can finally win through, although this thought of it all coming right acts as an image or dream to inspire us, rather than as a realistic expectation. It is like a distant horizon that we never quite reach, because the nearer we get to it the further it recedes.

This tension between hope and expectation, or between idealism and realism, is admittedly very difficult to maintain, both in theory and in practice. We can see this even in what must be the most confident area of Quaker intervention in the world, the testimony against violence and war. The original statement of 1660 reads as follows:

> We utterly deny all outward wars and strife, and fightings with outward weapons, for any end, or under any pretence whatever; this is our testimony to the whole world. The Spirit of Christ by which we are guided is not changeable, so as once to command us from a thing as evil and again to move unto it; and we certainly know and testify to the world, that the Spirit of Christ, which leads us into all Truth, will never move us to fight and war against any man with outward weapons, neither for the kingdom of Christ nor for the kingdoms of the world.

In its original context the testimony was clear and powerful. It was a refusal by the Quakers, 'the harmless and innocent people of God', to take up arms against the King or anyone else in the pursuit of their cause. They had come to realize that the kingdom of Christ - the utopian possibility that had seemed to come so close to realization in recent years - could not after all be brought about by violent revolution and civil war. It would be realized only by the use of 'inward', spiritual weapons which they had learnt to use and appreciate in their powerful missions and meetings throughout the country: means to awaken the conscience of people and inspire them to live differently. The refusal to use 'outward weapons' marked the peace testimony quite clearly, giving the Quakers too a clear identity as a nonviolent people - but only so long as they could remain as a people, relatively independent of the state and the rest of society. As soon as they became enfranchised politically and socially they became more active in society and they were able to influence even the policies of governments. In this situation a number of problems arose as to how the peace testimony was to be implemented, and more fundamentally as to what it now meant. For example:

1. How do we act as part of the State process, when the State inevitably depends on force and violence to maintain itself?

2. How do we work with others in the cause of peace (as we must) when they do not share our commitment to nonviolence?

3. Since we are now partly responsible for long-term activities, like the work of the European Community or the United Nations, how do we balance our personal principle with a consideration of long-term consequences?

4. How do we weigh up inner leadings and outer facts (analyses of conflicts, calculations of policy, risks attached to specific courses of action)?

5. How do we reconcile commitment to nonviolence with a commitment to save lives (e.g. with the UN aid convoys or 'policing' activities)?

These problems all point to a fundamental dilemma in our interpretation of the peace testimony today: how can we act in the world nonviolently when the world is still organized on the principle of violence (among other things)?

One response to this dilemma is to recommend that we should first of all be realistic, to go with the grain of the world, and find pragmatic ways of reducing violence in the world. But this is to ignore the spiritual basis of the testimony which is trust in a reality or power beyond the machinations of human beings, and commitment to a life that itself makes for peace. Another response to the dilemma therefore - the one adopted by most Friends, it seems - is to interpret the testimony as an absolute moral principle about the wrongness of war. This preserves the distinctive Quaker principle, but at the cost of encasing it in a fixed moral code. In confining our testimony to the institution of war in particular, and by construing it as a straightforward rejection of war, it seemingly fails to deal with the many and various dilemmas that violence continually presents to us, especially under the complex conditions of modern society.

The recent Gulf War is a case in point. It is now widely recognized that the war could have been avoided if enough pressure had been brought to bear on western leaders and the UN to implement sanctions. Quakers generally took the view - I include myself in this - that since sanctions were also violent to some degree, potentially at least, Quakers should not add to that pressure. Instead, they should insist that total nonviolence was the only possible option. However, insisting on this, as they and other pacifists did, gave the distinct impression to those who were listening that in the developing Gulf Crisis there were really only two options, total war and total nonviolence. If western leaders got the message at all, they would have drawn the conclusion that, since nonviolence was wholly unrealistic, war was the only real option. That was the conclusion they came to anyway, with or without our help. Did we really serve the cause of nonviolence best by making an absolute principle of it? There is a saying that the best is often the enemy of the good, which being interpreted in this context would mean that in making an absolute stand for peace we may have been contributing to the forces that made for war.

Early Friends may have been more realistic than we are, more able to balance the ideal and the real, or, as I put it before, to maintain the tension between hope and expectation. Reading the original testimony again I find that Friends were not advising the king one way or the other about the use of weapons, certainly not defying him or refusing him allegiance. On the contrary, they were strongly reassuring him that they, 'the harmless and innocent people of God, called Quakers', would not oppose him violently as they had his father, Charles I, when they had so enthusiastically supported Oliver Cromwell. This was a new commitment, which they in particular had been led to adopt as a matter of spiritual concern. It was not meant as a policy guide for government, which, as Isaac Penington said at the time, had not yet 'come into the gospel life and principle', and was therefore justified, according to its own principles, in 'defending (the people) against foreign invasions, or making use of the sword to suppress the violent evildoers within their borders'. But the wise Penington then added hope, as an inspiration to go out and help mend the world:

Yet there is a better state which the Lord hath already brought some into, and which nations are to expect and travel towards...[for] the gospel will teach a nation (if they will hearken to it) as well as a particular person to trust the Lord, and to wait on him for preservation.

Friends today could perhaps interpret their testimony as a witness to a way of life that can eventually do away with the need for violence and war. We can witness to this new possibility with every persuasion our words can muster, but most effectively, without question, by every effort we make to resolve actual conflicts nonviolently.

(Quotations from Horace Alexander, *The Growth of the Peace Testimony of the Society of Friends*, QPS, 1939/1982, pp.6,7. Historical details from Barry Reay, *Quakers and the English Revolution,* Temple Smith, London, 1985, ch.6.)

9. Building a commonwealth.

Another concern of Friends, second only perhaps to their concern for peace, is for 'sharing world resources'. And the spiritual logic is much the same. The humiliation and suffering of those who are deprived of the basic means of life seem to speak to Friends. It is an evil which touches their hearts, because Friends' faith and hope in this world are pinned on what humans fundamentally are and what they can ultimately do. They are led to care for the poor, not so much out of selfless, altruistic love - a rare enough gift anyway, when it is genuine - but out of a kind of sympathetic identification, believing that together our lives will make sense, whereas apart, in indifferent isolation, they become empty and meaningless. To 'walk cheerfully across the world, greeting that of God in everyone' is to make the connection that gives joy and significance to our lives as well. So, once again, God, as the mysterious source of our being, is mediated to us through other human beings, and vice versa, making human relations the great open field of our spiritual exploration.

From the very beginning of our movement Friends recognized that the humiliation of other human beings would have to be addressed politically. They recognized, as Penington put it, that nations lived according to certain 'principles', which, in the present state of things, tended to rely on violence and oppression as a way of maintaining order. If those who suffered violence and oppression, like the large numbers of poor in 17th century England, were to be given the dignity and freedom that were due to them the principles governing the nation would have to be changed fundamentally. They would have to come close to 'the gospel order' that Friends were trying in their own way to live by already. Unhappily, the attempt to achieve such a society under Cromwell - a 'commonwealth' in which the treasures of the earth would be justly shared - fell apart amid the endless bickerings of different religious groups as to what a gospel order should be like. In the disillusionment that followed Friends came to the insight that the commonwealth could come about only as a result of a much deeper transformation of people's lives and relationships. The political restructuring had to be backed up by and inspired by a spiritual awakening. The Society's commitment to nonviolence was part of that. But so too was the commitment to simplicity in life and honesty in business, which might be called the testimony on economics. It was not then unreasonable to hope, as Penington did, that the nation of England might soon arrive at that state, not least through the example and influence of Quakers.

It was not of course to be. But the question remains whether it is possible for us, some 300 years on, and with a gruesome history of economic misery in between, to go on believing in a commonwealth-to-come. The dilemma is similar to that around the peace testimony, which we framed as a question about how we can reasonably hope for a peaceful world when the 'principles' of the world rely so much on violence. If the temptation there is to make an absolute stand on nonviolence, leaving the outcome to God, the temptation here would seem to be to 'do our bit' for the poor and not worry too much about what difference that will make. I don't mean that as a criticism, as if there were another course of action that was all too obviously correct. There is a real dilemma here, and we all seem to be caught within it

- all of us, that is, who believe that a fair and just world must at least be possible. Quakers believe that because they believe that it is in the deepest interest of human beings to care for one another in a commonwealth, and it is within the resources of humans to respond to this insight with courage and determination - given the right circumstances. The problem is that the circumstances are now so stacked against us that it is impossible to see how we could ever realistically expect such a transformation of society. The 'principles' of the present world seem to be well and truly established: life is to be organized around a market, where money and profit rule, and policies at every level, from the local business to the European Community and the global economy, are to be geared to the maximisation of production and consumption. Little by little every human activity and institution is being gathered up into the maelstrom of an accelerating, competitive economy. And anyone who has any responsibility for running a concern, of whatever nature, is consumed with the question of how to survive economically. The appeal of such a system is blatant: it generates great wealth and at the same time gives people great freedom to consume this wealth. The cost however is horrendous: its ruthless competition leaves most people in the world impoverished, it devours natural resources to the point of exhaustion, it undermines the power of all human groups, the great nations included, to determine their own destiny, and it is so out of sympathy with people's real needs and aspirations that it is liable to falter or collapse at any time, as it is beginning to now.

In such a world we have to help our neighbour as best we can, which is already to go against the grain of this world's individualism. But it is ludicrous to imagine that helping out people here and there is going to make one bit of difference to the way the world works. The world system is now so immense, so complex, so fast-moving and powerful that it seems that nothing can stop it. So how are Quakers, with their unfashionable 'idealism', going to make a difference? And more importantly, how are they going to keep going on if they can't be confident that what they are hoping for and working for is actually still possible?

My proposal would be that the present crisis in the world economy, though very bad news in the short term, is good news in the long term. It confirms our insight that a market-led organization of life cannot ultimately satisfy human beings or make for peaceful relations; that on the contrary human beings will finally be satisfied only in a commonwealth. So in these dark times it might after all be possible to see a glimmer of hope, which ironically enough the 'darkness' enables us to see. Since the 'principles' of the present world are not sustainable, they must give way to something else, which is sustainable, which does harmonize the interests and needs of human beings. And with that possibility waiting to be realized, it does after all make sense to work for a fair and just way of living. Like Friends at the beginning of our movement, and perhaps like the first followers of Jesus too, we can try to anticipate the commonwealth, 'the peaceable kingdom', in the way we live now.

(For a fuller discussion of these issues see my *Global Theology*, SCM Press, 1990; and Ruth Tod et al., *Sharing World Resources: Which Ways Forward?*, QPS, 1988.)

10. Reclaiming the earth.

Much of this applies to the other great issue calling for action, the plight of the environment. Here too a seemingly unstoppable process of destruction is bending back on itself to destroy the human lives it was meant to serve. We are therefore being forced to rethink what we are doing to the environment by the palpable failure of what we are doing to achieve what it was intended to achieve. Obviously, the crisis of the economy and the crisis of the environment are very closely linked. But the second is making us rethink rather more deeply than the first. The first, we might say (following Fritz Schumacher), is making us rethink economics 'as if people mattered', which is something we have believed all along. The second is asking us to consider whether the belief that people matter is not part of the problem. I put it controversially to suggest how radical the questioning is. The point is that, in making people important, we in the west have nearly always made other living creatures less important, and sometimes of no importance whatever - except of course in so far as they might be useful to us human beings. This belief in the exclusive value of human beings has undoubtedly helped to fire the drive towards economic expansion which has characterized our western society over the last 500 years. And since this apparently unstoppable expansion is now causing a serious global crisis, it is inevitable that we should question this deep assumption about the unique value of human beings. To put it simply, we are learning through the crisis that if we don't value the earth for itself, rather than as simply a resource for us, we shall continue blindly to use it up, until we finally 'use up' the basis of our own existence. It is a new version of the old paradox that, to care for ourselves we have to care for others too, whereas if we care for ourselves exclusively we shall not finally succeed. The belief in the unique and exclusive value of human beings is some- times called anthropocentrism (putting humans at the centre), and many ecologists are now saying that the most important thing we have to do in this ecological crisis is to get rid of, or to 'transcend', this anthropocentric viewpoint.

Quakers have a fairly good record on the environment, compara- tively. But there is still a question about whether Quakers have gone through the rethinking required by the present situation. At a recent conference on the environment a well-known ecological scientist claimed that Christianity was largely to blame for the mind-set that had brought about the present crisis. In the question time that followed a Quaker asked whether he thought Quakerism might not be different in this respect. The answer was negative, because, he claimed, Quakerism was 'just as anthropocentric as other forms of Christianity'. (I won't quote his name, because I have it only on hearsay.) Is this true?

If it is true then we should have to conclude that Quakerism was making matters worse rather than better. We could reply immediately that of course the speaker knows very little about Quakerism if he imagines that its attitude to animals and plants has been no different to that of the mainline Christian churches. (On this see Keith Thomas, *Man and the Natural World: Changing Attitudes in England 1500-1800*, Penguin, 1985.) But this would be too hasty. The fact is that Quakers have been anthropocentric in their outlook. In a sense quite emphatically so. More than other Christians even, they have affirmed the dignity and resourcefulness of all human beings, because of 'that of God' within them, and they have not made a similar affirmation about animals and plants. In this respect, as I have emphasised before, Friends have been part of the humanising process of modernity, even when it took an undesirable turn, and they have in turn been influenced by it. It would therefore seem to be necessary for us to think again about this whole development and deliberately to distance ourselves from the modern, human-centred project. It is time to recover a sense of creation.

There are themes in our tradition which will help us to do this. On the basis of these we can develop a new understanding of the living earth which will make it possible for us to live in harmony with it, instead of continuing to live at odds with it. I would suggest five relevant themes (which I have written more fully on elsewhere, in 'Befriending the earth: a theological challenge', *The Friends Quarterly,* January 1990):

1. We are open to new light, from whatever quarter, and new leading from the Spirit, as circumstances change. We could now be sensitive to the earth and its creatures to gain a sense of how we should live in relation to them.
2. We can be aware of the hidden presence of God in all that God has made, not only in our fellow human beings. Perhaps the horizontal dimension of Quaker faith is now more important than ever.
3. We pursue our spiritual concerns through action as well as contemplation. We seek wholesome human relations, e.g. through active peace-making. We should do the same with

the earth. Perhaps the greatest challenge of the ecological crisis is the conflict-resolution between humans and the earth.

4. We have confidence in humans being able to respond to the light or the truth that is shown them, certainly when their own deep interests are at stake. The ecological crisis is speaking more and more clearly through the din of human chatter, and we need only to hope that it will be heard and heeded.

5. We have testimonies of peace, justice and simplicity, which, though they were first developed in connection with society, are now applicable to our relations with the earth. There is still a human commonwealth to be hoped for and worked for, not least for the sake of our environment. But there is also a 'common-wealth of creatures' (Augustine) which ecologists have been recently discovering. This too is to be cared for. But perhaps we should say that, given the close connection now between economy and ecology, there are not two commonwealths, but one new commonwealth of life.

CONCLUSION

11. The Quaker way.

Let's see if we can bring together the many issues we have been looking at in these ten studies and say something about Quakerism as a whole. How would we now want to describe Quakerism, in terms of its basic commitments? What is essential to it, and what is secondary or circumstantial? We have seen that it is fairly simple to say what Quakerism is *not*, because it was born in protest and still to some degree maintains that protest - against all forms of absolute authority, which, Quakers believe, always entails some oppression or violence of one sort or another. But what *is* it, positively? And what is it positively in favour of and committed to?

Let me suggest a positive account, by bringing together some of the conclusions I have come to on the more specific issues we have already discussed. I would suggest that Quakerism affirms

1. that human beings have within themselves the resources to find life's meaning and to fulfil it,
2. that life's meaning is found in one way or another in making connection with the source of life, mysterious though it is,
3. that we can begin to make this connection by becoming aware of the deepest feelings and intuitions within ourselves, below the level of words - silence is therefore a deliberate and necessary discipline in the spiritual quest
4. that awareness of this depth within ourselves makes us aware also of a deep bond with other human beings, however different they may be in other respects, so that our quest for meaning and truth is best shared with others,
5. that we best learn from others, including spiritual leaders of the past and of other traditions today, by recognizing in them the same spirit that moves us: that is, the same spiritual struggle and the same resource of light and liberation,
6. that we best meet the conflicts and concerns of everyday life by recognizing the spiritual potential of those involved, and by finding

practical ways to bring about a mutual recognition between them - which gives priority to mediation and nonviolent action, but does not provide hard-and-fast moral rules,

7. that we can live in hope because, whatever humans do to one another, or to the earth, it is still possible that they will come to recognize and love one another, which is the utopian hope of the 'peaceable kingdom' on earth.

These summary points provide the outline of a theological interpretation of Quakerism today. They are however only an interpretation, one way of making sense of the Quaker experience. They try to make explicit what is already implicit in Quakers' actual commitments. They do not represent what Quakers have generally said, much less what they have formally agreed to. And it would be ironical, to say the least, if they were taken to be statements that Quakers were supposed first to agree to before they could become members of the society. We should then have a Quaker creed after all! No, these are intended to illuminate, not stipulate, which, as I suggested at the beginning of this booklet, was the appropriate role for theological reflection in a Quaker context. We would be saying that, for example, when we gather in our silent meetings, minister to one another in our various ways, build community among ourselves or in the wider society, try to resolve conflicts in the world - when we do these things this is the kind of thing we are trying to do, this is the kind of faith-cum-hope that we bring to these activities and that sustains us through them.

This is not to say that we always have so much confidence in what we are doing. On the contrary, we may frequently doubt any one or all of the above affirmations (however we interpret them for ourselves), and feel we have little if any faith at all, in which case the meetings for worship and discussions with Friends become more occasions for searching than for finding. This is certainly true of many attenders, who are nevertheless fully a part of the meeting and its purpose. In these situations of uncertainty, which seem to be increasing at the present time, we may be wise to pare down our theological affirmation to something much more modest, more basic. We should perhaps say something like this: in such times Quakerism carves out a space where people who are anxious about the truth or meaning of their lives can come together and meet, and where together they can explore, discover and hopefully reclaim their truth. The faith is simply that together, in the silence, things can happen that enable us, miraculously, to discover ourselves and the way we have to go.